CORPORATE PSYCHOLOGY

COMPANY TRAITS

By-

SANJEEV SRIVASTAVA

5 / 356, Viram Khand – 5
Gomti Nagar
Lucknow (Uttar Pradesh), INDIA.

Cell No. ➔   917985948892

E Mail Id ➔ sanchapra@gmail.com

i

CORPORATE PSYCHOLOGY   COMPANY TRAITS

Copyright © 2012 Sanjeev Srivastava

All rights reserved.

ISBN-13:978-1981813377

ISBN-10:1981813373

DEDICATION

My Fathers –

MR (Brigadier) Tej Bahadur Srivastava, V.S.M. (Retired)

[LATE] Mr. Shyam Ji Singh

It is because of Almighty whose Blessings got this Book completed and Published. And then My Fathers encouragements were my Inspirations all the way along.

CONTENTS

Dedications   3

<u>Chapter 1</u>

<u>Introduction – Psychology</u>

In Ancient History, man was uncivilized and his only need was to quench his hunger for which he used to kill animals. His brain was primitive. In psychology, there is Id, Ego and Super ego. Id is that terminology in which man is like animal – senseless. He can't differentiate between maturity and immaturity. Whatever man wants his actions becomes that. Since man brain was primitive in Ancient History, his neurotransmitters in neurons were disturbed and imbalance were there in the secretions of these neurotransmitters which resulted in only certain specific types of neuron circuits in brain. This state of neurons system make up is categorical to children and even grown up man in that time were thus engulfed in Id psychology. Thus whenever man felt hungry, he used to pick anything kill animal and satisfy his hunger in a psychotic state of mentality particular to Id psychology. This era of stone-age continued and man slowly adapted to his mentality and psychology. With advancement of time man faced conditions like change in season, fear, death, birth, day and night, agony, pain, disease, light and dark, colors in nature and feelings and emotions which developed in him. Thus man apart from becoming expert in satisfying his hunger, he became advanced and his brain and psychology developed. He started differentiating in his actions, feelings and thoughts, his emotions became coherent to his fellow beings and thus in psychology there came Super ego which made him realize whether an action he must do or not. With this Super ego there also developed Ego in his psychology and thus he committed an action. Thus apart from learning differentiation in his actions as per Super Ego he committed actions also as per his Ego. Id, Super Ego and Ego is psychological specifics to man mentality. As we have seen, primitive man developed his psychology, man thus became different and he with increase in his population entered the phase of humanity in which he from his past expertise and experiences, he started creating new things and his brain developed with neurons having sophisticated circuits in brain and neurotransmitters giving signals to him which were scientists like. Thus man started dreaming and these dreams gave him visions. His psychology took a giant leap and he thus became engulfed in conscious, sub conscious states - man is in his sense in conscious state while in sub conscious state the unfulfilled desires of man are preserved which at times comes out as an outburst of his actions or in his dreams and sometimes he comes to a solution or compromise with situation for these desires in his dreams. In Super conscious state of mentality man is in a trance and his sixth sense becomes active which results in his contacts with Supernatural powers. Man learnt meditation to activate his Super-conscious state of mentality.

Chapter 2

Nervous System

Human beings Nervous System is made up of two parts – Central Nervous System and Peripheral Nervous System. Like Circulatory Systems blood vessels which are Artery and Vein, Nervous systems vessels are called nerves and in these nerves there are electrical signals flowing in forms of impulses. These impulses result in Actions after the man psychology permits. Central Nervous System (CNS) is made up of Brain and Medulla Oblongata. Peripheral Nervous

System (PNS) is made up of Spinal cord or Vertebral column and Nerves.

The basic unit of Nervous System is Neurons. Neuron cells diagrammatically are as under :-

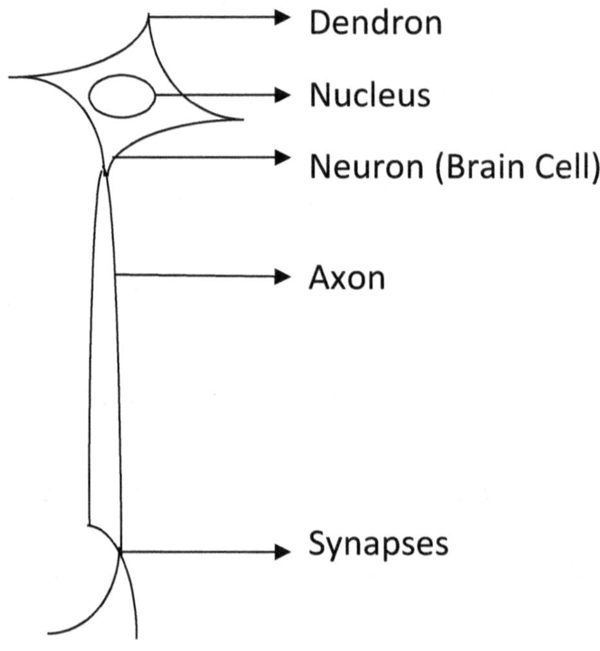

In the nucleus of these neurons are the genes where RNA and DNA are present in helical strands. Through these strands because of external and internal stimuli, signals are made which are combinations of Potassium (K) and Sodium (Na) chemicals and these chemicals have various combinations. These chemical combinations leads to formation of various kinds of secretions like dopamine and serotonin and such 150 and more types of secretions found in these brain neuron cells are called neurotransmitters. There are around 5 billion neuron cells in brain. These neuron cells through neurotransmitters controls the activity of the whole body.

The neurotransmitters through nucleus of neuron cells flows to axon and are fired which makes them reach synapses. Through these synapses where the dendrites of other neuron cells are present, these neurotransmission continues. This result in circulation of neurotransmitters and these sophisticated circuits of neurons develops brain.

In spinal cord there is a strand of spine which is thick rope like. Surrounding this spine is a number of vertebrae discs with marrow in it. These discs and spine through various kinds of signals in form of neurotransmitters received from brain; make a number of more signals which again is a combination of various kinds of chemicals but Potassium (K) and Sodium (Na) are the main chemicals. These signals then go to various nerves of the body.

There are two more kinds of nerves systems – Sympathetic and

Parasympathetic Nerves systems. These Nerves system are found throughout body and certain secretions like Acetylene, Adrenaline and more are found in these Nerves. These secretions gives various kinds of sense – see, touch, hear, taste, smell to body and also the sixth sense of supernaturalism. These nerve system is called Autonomic Nerve System and is present throughout body in a sophisticated circuit controlling involuntarily all the functions of visceral body organs and tissues. Various actions like digestion and excretion are certain involuntary actions which is the result of these nerves – The Autonomic Nervous System.

Thus we see that Central Nervous System, Peripheral Nervous System and Autonomic Nervous System are the components of Human Nervous System and Neurotransmitters. Adrenaline, Acetylene and other chemicals and secretions are present which are responsible for all voluntary and involuntary functions of a human body. The nervous system is active twenty four hours a day, thus nervous system finishes with the death of man. Man relaxes in his sleep, exercises, works and acts when he is awake. All these time, nervous system is active but at different levels. When man is sleeping then activity level of nervous system is less; while when he is awake and active then activity level of nervous system is more.

Nervous system of human being is the most complex in world and even the sophisticated circuits of supercomputers are no match for human nervous system.

Chapter 3

Human Psychology and Human Nervous System

The human nervous system through the flow of various secretions and chemicals through its nerves and cells are responsible for generation of impulses. These impulses give rise to various thoughts, feelings, emotions, desires, dreams, vision, foresight and actions. With the coming of these thoughts in Human mentality, the Human Psychology becomes active to commit an action. In the first stage, man starts feeling like an animal which is the Id stage. In this stage before man behaves like an animal and commits the action, his Super Ego Psychology which is overlapping Id Psychology becomes active which makes the man think whether he should commit the action or not. This gives him ample time to judge and formulate a plan for his action in Super Ego stage. Finally his Ego becomes active and he commits the action in this Ego stage of Psychology. Thus the impulse generation in nerves leads to thoughts and after some time of planning and judging, man commits actions.

It is an assertion to state that Human Nervous System is the Hardware of Computer and Human Psychology is the Software Packages of this Computer. Hardware or Human Nervous System is the creation of nature which a child gets during birth. As the child grows he through his senses learns new things which actually are the Software Package of Human Psychology. As the computer needs dust free and cool place for its functioning, similarly child needs an environment to learn and man needs an environment to work which are various School, Colleges, Universities, Home, and Society and Offices. These environments acts like a stimulation to Humans and his hardware and software thus activates his senses thus resulting in thoughts and actions. This way man adapts to various stimulations and his brain and actions becomes from simple to complex. With age man becomes sophisticated and a teacher to his children and youngsters. This result in the expertise of various faculties of Human Brain and Human Psychology and thus a variety of new things are created. We say then that it's a magnificent painting, amazing plot of film, genius, wonderful sight. With this expertise and creations, man gets the stimulation of praise and this result in creation of impulses along with more external stimulations; there are impulses produced in the gonads of Human Beings and thus Hormones are produced which are responsible in producing children who are more Handsome and Beautiful, Intelligent and Smart. This we can visualize through History. We see that Dark Age man was more like a monkey in appearance while today's man is Handsome. Also the Psychology of Dark Age was in particular Id while today man has a complex Psychology depending on his intelligence. Thus man through the process of evolution today has become the best creation of Nature. Because of this complex Nervous system and Psychology, Humans are on top of the chart of the various natures' living beings.

It has taken millions of years for Human

beings to achieve Modern age sophistication and in the coming years Man will become more sophisticated. Human Psychology will reach the peak of complexity and then man would be more like God where the Sixth Sense, Super consciousness and super Naturalism will become a matter of say in Human beings life. Man through his Psychology will commit actions in Super Naturalism. It will be an era where Human Nervous System as well will become more sophisticated in Neuron cells circuits and impulses which are not common in present era. Then there will be generated giving Super Natural powers to Human beings making him God like. Then Human beings will become more different in appearance and his views will be different resulting in Super Psychology era. At that time Psychology will require a different definition and new topics pertaining with Super Naturalism and Sixth Sense will be added in their Psychology. In this Super Psychology era man would be coming to know of God's existence and would realize a different perspective of life.

Chapter 4

Primitives to Corporatism

Man after developing his Psychology started becoming aware and realized the need of group. He came out of his caves and wandered long distances in group in search of food and to know what is there in his surroundings. He had to sleep in jungles, plain or on mountain hills when he wandered and thus his caves existence came to an end. He found such places better to live and also took to making small inventions through rocks, tree branches and metals like iron ore which he found in nature. Slowly he cleared jungles and made small huts from tree branches and mud and rock stones. These huts were like the caves where he used to live earlier. Thus huts development made the groups of these men to live in it. Slowly the sense of brotherhood developed in the group and man realized the importance of helping each other. There started developing a chain of friendship and man realized to create certain actions to express himself. Slowly, language developed and the human psychology took a giant leap thus giving new ideas to the grouped man.

Society developed gradually in the Ancient man and he developed a culture particular to a group. Certain groups worshipped stone, while certain groups were good in paintings, certain groups were good in hunting, certain groups developed in making huts. Thus specialization developed in ancient human groups. This led to development of specific faculties in human brain which created different impulses in different human groups. Thus men had human psychology in relation to his group and activities. Hunting group became brutes, ruling group became egoistic, physically strong group became victorious, weak group became docile and obedient. This way there generated a psychological differentiation in various groups which resulted in difference in thoughts, actions and culture.

With advent of psychological

differentiation, a need was felt in various human groups to take things from others and in return give things from whatever he had. This 'give and take' policy developed in these groups and this gradually brought commerce in limelight in ancient culture. 'Give and Take' process continued and then peoples became business like and invented the need of pricing which gradually led to 'Barter System' in groups. Thus 'Barter System' developed and man became more businesslike in his attitudes. Man in this 'Barter

System' also sold his services for which he was given something in return. Thus 'Barter System' led to the coming of places where small things of daily uses like pottery, ornaments, stone and iron weapons and many things were made. Men gave these things to others and in return took the things in a particular quantity specific to what he gave. This was 'Barter System' and from this era we see the sites of cottage industry in human culture. This is the base of modern era corporatism.

As time passed, man realized that he is paying price to others in his 'Barter System' in form of goods. His commerce and business attitudes of 'Barter System' were at peak. By that time Medieval History were round the corner. Man psychology developed certain new features like jealousy, killing others for his needs and desires, anger, sexual attitudes, sense of beautiful and handsome, prostitution, loose characters, dependency on wine and flesh. These kinds of psychology developed the foundation stones of

Kingdom and its specific culture where people lived under one ruler and worked to fulfill their needs and desires. These rulers were kings and they were imposing their whims not only in their kingdoms but also in the places which they won during war. This gave these rulers the psychology of egoism where their word and whims were law of the land. These rulers wanted to publicize their image and emphasize their superiority over others. Hence these rulers started in their kingdoms a new type of business pricing where coins with their embedded faces came in existence. We see this way as the beginning of pricing in 'Barter System' through coins. This resulted in giving coins to various services as a token of gesture called the price of these services or things. Thus 'Barter System' gave rise to 'Pricing System' in medieval history which is an important aspect in modern era world. 'Barter System' and 'Pricing Policy' continued together in medieval history with medieval society slowly discarding barter system and adopting pricing in their routine business.

It is to be noted that in ancient era, man used to make coins with pictures of God as per his visualizations embedded on these coins. Harappa Civilization man made such coins which through archeology have been found. However, in spite of the existence of such coins; there was 'Give and Take Policy' then. For doing small service or giving small things, the giver could walk away with pot full of such gold coins. This is specific to barter system. In short, there were no pricing; that is to say that no price was fixed for a particular service or a particular thing.

The fixation of price became advent in medieval era civilizations. Thus pricing on the basis of gold coins became a new routine in the business encyclopedia and barter era gradually finished.

With the extinction of barter system and advent of pricing, man in medieval history started giving value to every service and goods which he produced. There came in picture then richness and poverty and thus man realized the importance of gold coins or money. He started visualizing others in society and world as rich or poor. Various groups which had settled in various parts of world became kingdoms of various rulers and this made these kingdoms known by the name of their rulers. Peoples of these kingdoms interacted with each other and pricing became a new revolution in whole world's business. Gradually, rulers and their peoples started terming rich and poor peoples and rich and poor kingdoms in world. This led to the advent of 'Peer Psychology' and a feeling of 'My neighbor is rich while I am poor' developed in society. This peering of society brought a sense of accumulating more and more among the peoples of the world so that they become rich than their neighbors or friends or relatives. Even rulers were not spared of this 'peer psychology' and 'Superior than others Psychology'. They wanted to make their kingdoms richest and win the whole world in order to exhibit their Supremacy. Thus the rulers of whole world made their peoples form Army and fight wars. Those who won such wars made the losers their slaves and looted such kingdoms and exploited there peoples bringing a total disaster to such defeated kingdoms. There became a sense of glory, victory and defeat in whole world and peoples entered the psychology of enjoying their victory and mourning their defeat. Peoples became happy or gloomy and these attitudes of peoples finally led over a period of time to worries and tensions in their mentality with creation of mental illness among the peoples. These mentally ill peoples' genes became defective. In ancient era when peoples used to die, man could not understand such deaths and used to eat such dead peoples. Since people had Id psychology only then, their mourning were very brief but he never developed mental illness in that era because he had no sense of becoming tense over such deaths or for any events which were adverse to him. The advent of mental illness thus became a factor during wars of kingdoms by around medieval history. Such mentally ill peoples' defective genes led to their children becoming mentally retarded or defective suppressive genes in their cells which became dominant at later stage of life or in future generations. Mental illnesses came on medical map of humanity and there were Witch Doctors and Black Magic and a sense of God's anger or some angry spirit and ghosts; came in limelight. Peoples could not understand this kind of illness which was actually a distortion of diseased peoples' psychology and brain. Medieval History and Defective Psychology continued and then came an era of 'Scientific Revolution' in World. Many new Machineries and

Technologies were invented and many new practices and lands were discovered. It became an era of Creation.

The rulers became comprehensively dictators and a new terminology – 'Taxation' was developed by them in which peoples from his earnings had to pay a part of it as rulers share. The rulers used this part of tax to make roads, wells, buildings and temples, build army and run his kingdom. However ruler became so engrossed in taxing the peoples that these peoples revolted against such rulers. 'The Russian Revolution', 'The French Revolution', 'The British Revolution', 'The American Revolution, 'The Indian Revolution' are exemplary Revolutions of such Kingdoms People's Revolt. Human Civilization entered the phase of Modern Era and 'Kingdoms' were re-termed as 'Nations' of the World. In this modernization of world, there was an overall advancement in the various societies of the World. Certain Societies and Nations of the World advanced to such an extent that their barbaric attitudes gave rise to 'Dictator Psychology' as per which they wanted to win whole World. This Dictate led to two World Wars and creation of 'League of Nations' and finally 'United Nation Organization'. Also every Nation formulated its own Constitution, Boundary, Law and Society and all this led to National differentiation of World. Man also developed Medical Science to know more about himself.

With above mentioned advancement in Society of World, terms like industry;

goods; products; laborers; workers came in picture. The whole world became a mass of people's population from few groups of the ancestors of these peoples in ancient era. The needs of peoples grew. This created places in World where goods were produced to cater the needs of World population. Such places are the shapes of ancient era cottage industry. Today these industries are a big land of production unit through various machineries and such factories have become common throughout World. It is worth to mention that 'Scientific Revolution' in

Medieval History took place in Britain and with every new invention a factory were made to produce these inventions in mass scale for World Population. This made Britain World's Richest Nation and because of the sale of its factories products throughout globe Britain adopted the strategy of Market capturing of World which led to establishing of companies in almost all kingdoms of the World. Thereafter, Britain through manipulations exerted its supremacy over world kingdoms and finally captured them as result of which it is said that 'The Sun never sets in British empire'. Whole world because of Britain's Industrial revolution or the scientific revolution became a part of British Kingdom. However, whole world witnessed peoples' revolt and today Britain has lost all its victorious nations. In today's world almost all nations are independent.

It is categorical to state that after 'Second World War' and 'United Nation Organization' formation; whole world has been divided into Advanced or

Developed Countries and Developing Countries. Developed Countries are the richest in world and they are giant corporate nations with factories in abundance and mass production of goods for whole world. This has given rise to the term corporate which is a vaster sense of industry. Today, there is a rise of this corporate sector in world with people in these corporations producing goods and giving their services to their customers.

Chapter 5

Corporate Sector – Production and Services

In Modern age, Corporate Sector has been divided into Production units and service units. Production units produce mass of goods called products while service units provide various services to their customers. Developed Nations are Corporate Giants like USA, France, Russia, U.K., Germany, and China. Developing Nations are developing their corporate sector like India, Malaysia, Thailand, Mauritius, and Indonesia.

Production units are divided into various kinds which are described here. Cottage industries are basically in villages where products are produced related to agriculture and pottery. Small Scale Industries are industries where production and number of workers are limited. They have one or two machines and are basically opened in outskirts of town. Their pollution level is low. Examples of such industries are plastic industry. Medium Scale Industry have greater amount of production and their workers are limited to 50 workers. They have a turnover of around Rs. 5 crores per annum. Large Scale Industries are big industries where more than 50 workers work and production is on mass scale. Moreover, their turnover is above Rs.5 crores. Proprietorships are those units where whole industry is owned by an owner and he is the sole in-charge of his factory. He has to pay Government tax and his product must be as per Government standards. For all his factory decisions only the owner is responsible. Partnerships are such organizations where the owners are more than one person and the whole production unit is jointly the responsibility of these partners. The partners as per their share in the industry have that kind of share in the profits. Private Limited organizations are those organizations where the Government has a limited hold on such organizations. Government has formulated certain company laws. These laws are imposed on such organizations to an extent. Limited organizations are the organizations where Government laws are enforceable on all the staff, owners, workers and products. Certain laws like pollution law, water tax, electricity tax, property assessment and income tax, product standardization law, leave, gratuity, funds, salary, number of workers, safety standards for factory and workers – all such laws under company law including Accounts assessment are enforceable by government through their Ministry of Industries. Private sector organizations are owned by industrialists while public sector organizations are owned by governments of various nations.

Multinational corporations are such organizations where they have production units and offices in more than one nation. Autonomous organizations are such which have both public and private sector designs, that is to say that government has little say in the affairs of such organizations. Cooperative industries are such where a group of organizations form a union and their own laws which are agreed by the government. The goods produced by all above mentioned production units have a value and are sold for a price to their customers.

Service units have also come up in a big way in the corporate world. Schools, colleges, universities, institutions, academies are present throughout world providing education to students from all walks of life. The teachers and professors are paid salary for the knowledge which they impart to their students. Coaching institutes and tutors also come under this service unit. Hotels and resorts are places where customers are served food and enjoy sightseeing. Restaurants and picnic spots are the places where this facility is present in small scale. Hospitals are places where patients are kept and given medicines by Doctors. Nursing staff in such hospitals provide care and attention to such patients. Clinics are also there where Doctors attend outdoor patients for which he gets a fee. Lawyers also provide legal services to their clients. Banks are money houses where peoples keep their money for an interest. There are big financial institutions which float bonds for which the bondholders get interest.

These service units may be owned by peoples under private sector or government under public sector and offices. There are trusts and autonomous organizations which also provide services to their clients.

Today, from needle to satellites are the outcome of production and service units under corporate sector and on the basis of this corporatism of nations; world is divided into corporate giant developed nations and developing nations. The currency value depends on the corporate sector of a nation.

Chapter 6

Corporate Workers Familiarizing

In corporate world, even the owners are workers and are designated as Managing Directors or Chairman. Then there is Joint Managing Director who also makes management decisions. Down the ladder are Directors who are specializing in various fields of production or service. These Directors may be Director (Production), Director (Technical), and Director (Administration). President and Vice

President are designated after corporate elections. There are Trade Unions and Union leaders who have a grouped say in management decisions. Since time immemorial there has been fight between management and trade unions. Trade unions comprise of all the workers of the company and these workers fight for their rights against the management or owners of the corporation. These workers in the trade unions elect their leaders or representation and they are president or vice-president and office bearers of the trade unions. Workers are basically labor class who may be foreman, fitters, electrical man, and factory or machine engineers. Because of these workers, goods are produced by the machines in factories and mills. Then there are managerial staffs like Regional Manager, Zonal Managers, General Managers, Marketing Managers, Accountants, Administration Managers, Receptionist or Front Office Staff, Public Relation Staff, Human Resource Manager, Company Secretary, Cost Accountants, Chartered Accountants. Under them are the

Executives, Officers and Assistants who execute orders. Financial Analysts are there who formulate budget for various departments of the organizations. Corporate giants have a huge publicity and events organization department which are responsible for the propaganda of such organizations. These organizations have their own research departments where a number of engineers from different technological fields work. Today many corporations have their medical clinics and teaching schools in their vast campus. The infrastructure is also fast developing along with advent of new technologies. Then there are clerical staffs like typists, computer – fax – telex operators, peons, mess staff and canteen staff. It is therefore evident that in good corporations, we find almost whole world in a nutshell and a large number of peoples are working who for their production and services are paid salaries which is the sole means of their livelihood.

In Service units, the peoples who give services to the clients are basically educated and thus the service units can be said to be the Intellectual class of nation. They are well educated, highly qualified and give their consultations for a fees. This class is from all walks of life. They are a respectable group of peoples and are intelligent. They help peoples in their problems and solve these problems. They may also motivate peoples. In service world, we find teachers, professors, tutors, bank employees, hotel workers, doctors, engineers, researchers, managers, travel agents, consultants, scientists, plumbers, fitters, mechanics, drivers and cooks or servants.

Chapter 7

Psychology in Corporate Sector

Modern age is an age of cut throat competition where excellence, quality and quantity have the supreme say in society. Peoples work and if their work is appreciable then they are on top of the ladder while those whose work is not good; they struggle for excellence otherwise they remain on the bottom ladder as dissatisfied with their life. So peoples have educational qualifications and practical experience so that they provide the best of their services. There is a sense of achievement in today's society where peoples count the number of their qualifications and years of their practical work experience in order to prove their excellence in modern society. Apart from this excellence, there is a sense of creation and peoples want to do new things in society which no other people have done in past so that such creative peoples in society have an easy access to popularity and fame. There is a new psychology in today's society which is manipulative delusions very similar to hypnotism. Peoples show off and talk big about themselves in order to create an impression among others. They manipulate facts and create a false impression in peoples mind in order to earn big money. Such peoples have fraudulent tendencies and can be said as psychological patients similar to Psychosis.

Since there is lots of competition, peoples have four problems in the corporate world which are temptations, tension, anxiety, and fear.

In the materialistic world, the corporate worker is always tempted to change organizations for a better salary and better designation. He wants money for which he becomes tempted even to do illegal works in organizations like bribing or killing trade union leaders or committing fraud. Temptations are present in the whole corporate world as a source of discontent with their life. Next is tension in the corporate world where every worker is worried to produce result. If result is 100% from their work, then such workers get praise and rise in their salary and their confidential report is good. Such workers whose result is not good – they get worried and become tensed to complete their work. They don't want to spoil their records or get demoted or have a cut in their salary. So they become tensed. Tension is a common cancer in corporate world because this tension is responsible for various psychiatric and addiction illnesses like frustration, depression, wine and cigarette, drugs, prostitution and often in this tension, we find peoples becoming psychotic.

They require the help of a psychologist and a psychiatrist. Anxiety is common in corporate workers because these workers are always anxious for achievements in life and their career. They lose the value of time and cannot wait. They have money and they want immediate return from their money and if there is any delay, the peoples become anxious. Anxiety is a problem for which the help of a psychologist is a must. Fear Psychosis or Phobia is another problem in corporate sector where peoples are always under a kind of phobia of losing their jobs. They have a fear that they will be fired from their job by senior authorities and then they will become unemployed and will not get other job. To avoid such a circumstance, employees are either docile and obey all orders of their management or form trade unions and become its members so that they don't lose their jobs. This phobia of losing jobs is also a very common psychology of employees of the corporate world.

Man has become competitive and materialistic in corporate world. There are a variety of opportunities and this often creates confusion in the society. Peoples have to choose a field for their specialization and after a while they get bored in their work which is monotonous. At such stage of their career, they again take up another specialization course and again spend time educating them. Today there are combinations of various courses which mean that employees have to do two or three courses for a particular work. This has led to confusion among the students while selecting their field of specializations.

With advance in all curriculums of professional education, it is seen that youngsters have to put in lots of efforts to complete their educations which makes them book worms. Such youngsters are physically weak and wear spectacles and might be a man with defective mentality. It is evident that corporate employers take lots of work from their employees. They keep long working hours including overtime works. Employees have also to do intensive touring in their jobs. All this leads to very little time or no time with employees for themselves or their families. So society has come up with new psychology of fatigues' of these employees which may lead to various heart and circulation diseases. Employees in the phase of work do not pay proper attention to their health which is fatal. There are accidents happening in factories where workers lose their hands and other organs in machines because they are fatigued which leads to carelessness and alertness becomes less. It is a must that such employees visit a psychologist and learns the techniques to relax and sleep. There are Relaxation exercises and through hypnotism, such employees can sleep and relax and regain their carefulness and alertness.

In present world, we find exodus of population from villages to cities and developing nations to developed nations in search of jobs especially in corporate sector which provide lucrative and easy money. By easy money, it is meant that even peoples who are less educated and school or college dropouts can find jobs in factories at junior posts at good salaries and such youngsters specialize in such small works. It is another problem for modern society because for such class of employees who are easy suspect to delusions; it is very difficult for psychologists to remove their delusions. Such employees require the help of Psychiatrist and medicines for they become schizophrenic or violent with manic attitudes. It is very important to give basic education and give proper awareness to this section of workers. These workers are basically fascinated by the glamour of big cities and rich nations and in a state of this charmed glamour; they reach such places while in reality they are unfit to take jobs in such places. They are easy prey to sweet and spicy talks which the job brokers have with them for money. These peoples are cut away from reality.

In corporate world, there are talks like efficient worker and productive work. Such talks praise employees and employees must be efficient and productive. Dullness or pinching talks or firing by managers spoil the efficiency of the employees and his productivity decreases. Therefore, it is a must that such employees realize their shortcomings through self-analysis and in future, avoid all mistakes and improve their efficiency. They can take the help of a Psychologist for self-analysis.

Employees at junior posts who are less educated have a greater level of job satisfaction. By job satisfaction it is meant that employees like their job and do not want to change his organization. This job satisfaction gives a sense of well being to the employees and he does his job with full efficiency. Senior employees want more and more money and better infrastructure and so remain dissatisfied with their jobs. Their job satisfaction is less and they remain discontent with their jobs. Such employees change their jobs frequently. So workers remain happier with their jobs while senior managers remain less happy with their jobs.

In modern era, there is a population explosion and government or private sector is unable to provide jobs to the masses. There is thus the term unemployment very common in modern society. The unemployed educated section of society is a burden on their family. Such sections of peoples are frustrated and depressed. They are discontent with their life and have suicidal tendencies. They even after getting jobs are dissatisfied with their jobs because it is a junior position. Such peoples' experiences are practically nothing and so corporate world gives them junior positions to gain experience. But unemployed peoples in their depressive mood don't like such junior posts. It is a must that these kind of employees remove such attitudes from their behavior with the help of a psychologist through comprehensive counseling and take up such posts full heartedly. They should stick to such jobs, gain two to three years experience and then go for high designation jobs.

In corporate world, there is

monotonous of job environment, that is, same work routine is followed day after day and year after year. This monotonic job makes the workers bored after a period of time. To avoid this boring attitude, workers should take leave and enjoy sightseeing or picnic to change his mood. He may also take up new courses to enhance his qualification and work. All this will change the mood of workers. It is a must that workers know how to enjoy and change their boring mood.

<u>Chapter 8</u>

<u>Interpersonal Relation and Challenging Environment</u>

In Corporate World, interpersonal relations play a major role in communications. There may be Worker – Worker, Manager – Worker, Manager Executive, Male Staff – Female Staff, Owner – Worker, Owner – Female Staff, and much such type of interpersonal relations. Such kind of relations are fruitful because in such interpersonal relations there are communication of ideas, worries of career and life, talks of working environment and infrastructure and many views are thus shared. An organization with good and cordial interpersonal relations always prospers because all the employees know each other and feel homely. They live as brotherly team and put in their best for their organization. It is also seen that certain Male Staff – Female Staff interpersonal relations have culminated in marriage and such couples married life is happy and successful. Even Trade Union leaders and Owners interpersonal relation – if it is a happy relationship with an attitude to help each other then such organizations prosper to enormous heights.

In service units, interpersonal relations have been limited to matrimonial attitudes. A Doctor gets married to a Lady Doctor and likewise. However, a sense of brotherhood is present to a lesser extent in Service unit. The helping attitude is not much because peoples think that in this competitive

World if they help someone then he or she will become above him. Thus a selfish attitude is more prevalent in Service units.

Corporate World – both Production and Service sector is having a very challenging environment and everyday peoples apart from monotonous jobs, face certain new things in their jobs. These new aspects of jobs is like a challenge to the workers or employees or peoples in service units. To cope up with the new challenges, the employees have to utilize all their practical expertise and professional knowledge and also have to consult their seniors. This way they learn how to face the new challenges and improve their caliber. There is a variety of such challenges and almost daily employees face such challenges.

Today in the fast changing World, new environment, laws, works, infrastructure and so on are coming up which gives a variety of new challenges to the society. Peoples are finding difficulty in coping up with these new challenges. Though they learn many things from these challenges but they don't become experts and so after a while they forget how they had tackled the problem. To avoid this forgetting tendency, peoples must write their experiences in a diary and keep it safe for remembering purposes. They should sharpen their memory through meditations.

Society is a nutshell of interpersonal relations and challenging environment in corporate world and both production units and service units have learned many new things from all challenges which it is facing.

Chapter 9

Women in Corporate Arena

A girl is a child, sister, daughter, wife, mother, friend and relation of a man. It is therefore essential to educate girls so that she provides a healthy life to man. It is said that girls are the respect of a man. A man has respect as far as the girls of his family are good. The moment the girls of a family adopt to lose characters, the men of such family loose respect in society. So education, healthy environment, good thoughts, good attitudes of life, good characters are a must for every girl so that she becomes a respectable woman in society.

Today's woman is fast learning all new things which are coming in modern society. Women are becoming educated and do not limit their life to the four walls of the house. We find women working in almost all walks of professional life. Women have not spared corporate sector as well and we find women becoming managers or doctors or engineers. However, in spite of such professional jobs, women still look forward to marriage and man's security. Marriage is thus a very important happening of every professional woman as well. This marriage is a pious bondage of every woman with man and therefore if a professional woman gets married, it is really a Godly pious event in society.

In Corporate World, women are coming in a big way from junior level typists, computer workers to senior posts like Managers and Directors. In service unit women are seen becoming Doctors, Hotel and Bank staff, Engineers, Architects, Manageress, Industrialists and so on. Such Women earn and their earnings are definitely a big helping hand to their family. Such women get good match in their marriages and are happy with their life. However, with professionalism of women, we have witnessed women having opposite sex friends whom they wish to marry. There is a conflict in family related to such a situation in modern society. It is a must that modern society changes their attitudes towards women and allows such marriages. As man can choose girls, so girls should also have the authority to choose their partners. Girls with boyfriends if are earning, society should allow such marriages irrespective of caste, creed, culture and above all horoscope.

Corporate women dreams of doing big things both for her organization and family. She is job satisfied and seldom change job. Women remain in an organization for a longer time and are more loyal to their organizations. She seldom indulges in fraudulent activities and is more God fearing than their men counterparts. Women employees do their jobs for a fixed working hour and she seldom works overtime or in night hours. Girls want to work in day hours from morning till evening for in them there is sense of fear of getting raped by their male bosses. Such a fear is very common in corporate sector women staff. Corporate women tend to specialize in one field and know her job properly. She does not like firings in her jobs.

Chapter 10

Children in Corporate Arena

Children working at a tender age from 6 years to 14 years have raised political and social eyebrows round the globe. Such children are less privileged and instead of enjoying their childhood in happiness; they lead their life working in offices, mines, factories, construction sites; as laborers and small workers. Such children life is a total misery and their education comes to a staggering or total halt. The employers pay very little to such children in spite at times, taking work from them fit for an adult. Such children are daily exploited and sexually abused. A type of phobia is created in the brains of such children in which they fear their senior authorities and owners. They mostly become hysterical and have weeping tendencies. The psychology of such children whose Id phase has just finished and ego and super ego phase is not fully developed, it is seen that such children life are not fully civilized and they are more animal like.

Children in corporate arena gets very little care and attention in their employment and at home. Thus their psychology is very much defective and they gain a Rough attitude in their behavior where there language is rough and less polished and their dressing style is unhygienic while their appearance is pathetic. They have a bad hygiene like they may go to toilet or may not brush their teeth. Such children may shave occasionally when they grow up. Thus their hygiene is totally spoilt and they don't listen to others to improve their hygiene. Thus the appearance of such children looks like that of Ancient age man and such children become used to exploitation and sex. Since these children are uneducated, they don't know how to express themselves and their actions are thus very peculiar to that of madness. Such children have to sleep on floor and stay in congested places where there is no light and ventilation. This leads to various types of skin diseases in such children.

Such children's life is thus limited to the

place of their stay and place of their work. Even girl child workers life is as miserable as boy child workers. Only difference is that girl child workers are more sexually abused than boy child workers. Thus these children spend their gonads. This becomes as the main source of their entertainment in their habits and various sexual diseases gets to them which leads to a psychology of these children particular to open sex. For them body is to make fun and play with its organs. It is very difficult to treat such children.

Both Psychologist and Psychiatrist face lifelong problems treating such children. The delusion and psychosis of such children is to such an extent that such children are mad and not in their civilized sense. It is a must to educate such children and create a sense of well being in these children. Such children must become aware of the world and change their attitude towards their life. Proper care and attention and medical and psychological attention must be given to such children.

Chapter 11

Money Value in Corporate Arena

Society today is Rich or Poor as per which World is divided into Developed Nations (Rich) or Developing Nations (Poor). Today everybody and everything is having a price. This price defines the Money Value of a product or any service. So a product is expensive article or a product is cheap article and same goes as expensive service or cheap service. Based on the price or Money value of products and services there are Stock Exchanges which determine the 'Price Index' of a Nation and if 'Price Index' is high that Nation is rich while a low 'Price Index' Nation is poor.

In Corporate Sector both product and service plays an important role. A product or service is of very good quality and so its price is high while the same product or service is of low grade and so its quality is poor and its price is low. Based on this theory, in developed nations we find very good quality and so the prices are very high and so such nations products are good and expensive. Developing Nation Corporate produce same goods or services but of subsidized quality and so its prices are low. So Developed Nations because of high Money Value have a very high standard society where peoples pay any price for any standard product or services. Such peoples have a materialistic view in their psychology for anything. Even the corporations are very rich and they pay very high salary to their employees. Materialistic psychology is so intense in such high paid employees that they think that everything can be bought from God till death. They have less compromising tendency because they have money and they get their things done at no time. In Corporate sector of developing nations corporate sector have substantial infrastructure and peoples are getting very less salary which is just sufficient for their livelihood. The employees thus have a different view towards life and they compromise with various situations happening in their life. They however have faith in God and take money as necessity of life but not everything in life.

'Peering Psychology' is very intense in corporate arena of both developed nations and developing nations. If an employee is highly paid then his colleagues and junior employees try to improve their efficiency and market value so that they also come in the category of highly paid employees. 'He is rich and I am poor' thus plays a very important psychology role in corporate arena and thus struggling tendency comes in poor employees so that they improve their money value in the corporate world.

Today Money value or Price has come up in a very big way in corporate world. Even Governments bows in front of the money value of the corporate sector. Privatization is done in almost every nations and a day will come when it will be corporate money world.

<u>Chapter 12</u>

<u>Infrastructure and Glamour of Corporate</u>

Corporate World has the major chunk of world money. It provides all modern infrastructures to its employees both in office and at home. Phone, Fax, Telex, Computers, Robots, Car, Accommodation, Air Conditioned offices, Lucrative salaries, arranged office environment with clean hygienic toilets — name any facility and corporate world provides it. Thus both home and office environment is very congenial and peoples work efficiently.

The corporate with better facilities and infrastructure will have better employee's production and efficiency. Today machine have come which are totally automatic and it is every employees production and efficiency. Mostly employees from technical field dream to work on such machines. An employee getting excellent infrastructure facilities doesn't wish to leave such an organization till he retires. Thus employees stick to such corporate organizations anywhere in the whole world.

It is seen that in Developed Nations Corporate Giants are present where all sorts of infrastructure and facilities are present. In such Giants, it is seen that employees seldom leave them. Their efficiency and self esteem is very high and they are more content with their jobs. In those corporations where infrastructure is limited, there employees dropouts are more and they are less content with their jobs, such employees if less educated would stick to these organizations and employees with better qualifications and experience struggle in such organization network till they get their dream corporation.

Corporate world conducts lots of cultural programs, sports events and media programs. All these events have glamorized corporations. Employees are attracted first to such corporations which are more glamorized. Such glamour gives a fascinated image to youngsters and an impact come in their psychology which is that of 'Corporate Brand'. Thus they know corporations through its product and through their events. Such kind of 'Brand' impact goes deep in the psychology of youngsters as well as its employees and they become staunch admirers of such Corporations and for which they put in their best of efforts to join such organizations. Thus a 'Corporation Craze' can be seen in youngsters, aspirants and employees of such corporate glam-ours. If an aspirant is unable to join his choice corporation then he becomes frustrated and struggles a lot to join his dream corporation. He will not be a satisfied employee till he joins his choice job and corporation.

Thus we see that both corporate infrastructure and corporate glamour has a 'Craze Impact' on aspirants and its employees. Such peoples though doesn't need any kind of psychiatric treatment or psychological guidance but if they are frustrated for a long period of time and have a depressive psychology then they must compromise with the situation and consult good psychologists for counseling. They may require medical help as well.

Chapter 13

Sex and Drugs Abuse in Corporations

Corporate produce goods and services in mass scale as a result of which employees have to work long tiring hours. They become a fatigued mentality and wish to remove their tiredness. For this they enjoy programs or through media world or going on a sightseeing tour. However, it is seen that such employees have money and their character because of their richness become illusive. They through media programs where they witness sex and drug abuses, enters their psychology as they see in Media. There are lots of sex films in market by the name of Blue Films. In rich nations such films demand is very high while in developing nations such film demands is on the increase. Employees after seeing sex films in their homes and offices develop a mentality to enjoy sex and for this their Ego permits because they feel that if films can be made on sex then why can't they enjoy sex that way, thus they become delusive and see world as sexy world. Sex in their brain and body heat their Super Ego in spite of telling them that they shouldn't go for multiple sex, peoples ego still permits and so they womanize. Employees in rich nations where open sex is a routine also spend a part of their salary enjoying sex. There are Cabarets Houses and Pubs where sex is very common.

Peer force has a very big effect in corporations. Because of 'Peer', employees come in the grip of drugs and they abuse it to such an extent that their hospitalization becomes essential. Drugs like Smack, Heroin, Tablets, Injections, Charas, Brown Sugar, Opium's, LSDs and Viagra are common drugs. Then there are Alcohols and Wines which also comes in drugs category. Employees because of confusion and peer force become delusive and think that if they drug themselves they would become big and God. Such employees begin with cigarettes and tobacco and finally are led to take bigger drugs. They enjoy drug kicks and they wish to remain in it.

Drug use of any kind from smoking (cigarettes) to Water drugs (Alcohols) to solid particles (Tablets) is becoming very common in corporate world.

It is seen that both Men and Women employees are victims of tiredness and both take to Sex and Drugs abuse – some do it openly while others do it in hidden. This is a disease as per United Nations – WHO. Both Addictions and Sex are becoming great problems in modern society. No strata of society is free from this abuse and it is thus a problem which even Political World is not neglecting because a large section of society masturbate and in open sex society peoples are happy with open sex – lots of gay society organizations, brothels and cabarets houses have come up through Government Licenses. Here even child is sex abused.

Chapter 14

God Perception in Corporate World

Employees in Corporate World are engulfed in materialism. All their work gets done because of their lucrative salary and contacts. They enjoy a luxurious life and everything is within their easy reach. Thus it has become a tendency in employees of corporate world to do whatever they wish to do. A big chunk of such employees are Atheist and they challenge the very existence of God. They don't pray God or Meditate. For them money is everything. Apart from buying heart and death, they buy almost everything which they wish. They do any kind of work; such kinds of employees don't care for emotions and feelings and are money blinds. They thus are mostly authoritative, stubborn and arrogant and bold.

However there is a smaller section of corporate society who prays God when they are free. They may pray once a day or once in a week when they visit Church, Temple or Mosque. This section of corporate world has a mixed feeling towards God and they go to Temples especially when their important work is stuck somewhere. Such peoples pray to God to get their work done. It is like bribing God through such prayers and they believe that their work will be done. Such employees are selfish in their attitudes and utilize their money after lots of thinking.

There is the next section of Society which is Theist and Pray God and

Meditate. This section of employee is very less and such employees pray God with all heart following all steps of their prayers. They pray daily and are happy in their attitudes. Such employees are God fearing and do not indulge much in illegal activities. Their Super Ego and Ego psychology is very strong and they at time become staunch follower of a particular God or particular religion. This staunchness is a delusion and such employees must consult a psychologist for proper counseling to remove their delusive staunchness. Everybody is free to any religion and everybody is God and God is everybody this they must understand and must respect all religions.

A lesser number of Corporate World prays to God for money and all happiness of life. Such peoples pray daily in morning and evening. Such peoples are of passive mentality towards God and spiritualism. They don't hurt anybody and do their work efficiently. They believe in God and their work.

Next it is seen that certain number of Corporate World pray to Satan the Devil God. Such employees are of violent attitude and can believe in black magic and witchcraft. Such peoples are of violent attitude and can become dangerous in their working environment. They believe in money power and killings. They indulge in all sorts of illegal activities and such employees are psychotic. They require medical care of a Psychiatrist.

<u>Chapter 15</u>

<u>How to Judge Personality of a Corporate</u>

Corporations have come up in a variety of fields and both its Production unit and service unit have a number of highly qualified staff. To judge the Personality of such staff, first a psychologist must ask their qualifications. Certain employees are having fraud qualifications and such persons will not be able to answer properly the educational qualification questions. Next their practical experience questions related with their job and infrastructure environment should be asked. Usually employees answer such questions with great accurateness. Then to judge their intelligence, IQ test – both verbal and non verbal must be conducted. It is found that employees are able to answer such questions. Then Block Test and Puzzle Tests should be conducted in which there is a block with various wooden figures and the employees must be asked to arrange these figures in block and complete it. There are certain puzzle tests like two identical figures and employees must be asked to find differences in the figures. After judging the IQ, it is must to judge flight of ideas or imagination in which there are tests like Thematic Appreciation Test (TAT) and Word Appreciation Test (WAT). Both TAT and WAT will give a clear picture of the psychology of a person. In TAT there are 10 pictures and 1 blank card and employees are asked to write a story on the cards pictures. Similarly in WAT a number of words usually around 50 words are given to employees and they must be asked to write their first reaction. It is found that many employees will be able to complete this test and exhibit a good degree of imagination which means that they are fit for challenging jobs where they can use their creative imagination. Next the Psychologist must subject the employees to 'Managerial Aptitude Test' to judge the management qualities of the employee and find whether such an employee is fit for higher Management posts or not. This test usually many employees at junior posts are unable to complete because their awareness and practical experience is still in the learning stage. In this test, there are around one hundred fifty or two hundred questions related with management and practical experience of the employees. High designated employees will come out with flying colors in this test. Finally, there is 'Rorschach Test' in which Ten Cards are shown and these cards are having abstract pictures in black and white as well as colored. The employees' way of answering and what he answers is seen and his mood is also seen. Based on this test a comprehensive judgment can be made of the employees. It would be found that 'Lack of Security' and 'Flight of Ideas' would be found in many employees based on 'Rorschach Test'. Psychologist must also ask the employees to write a complete picture about their life and thoughts in a note book and he must interview the employees in which he can ask certain specific questions about employees. This also gives a comprehensive judgment about Corporate Personality.

Chapter 16

Corporate Psychology

'Corporate Psychology can be defined as the impact of any kind which a corporation creates in the minds of peoples. The impact may be ranging from good, average, bad or events image or brand image or its employees image and behavior'.

'Corporate Psychology' is a new concept and in 'Developed Nations' — Corporate Giants use all sorts of publicity propaganda to give an image of awe about their products in the minds of masses. 'Developing Nations' Corporations are now coming up with lots of publicity propagandas. These propagandas are such that Corporations spend a major chunk of their profits on it. We see lots of Advertisements of Corporate products in Media World. Corporations have a department – events management and Public Relations Department related with Mass Communications. This department conducts 'print and electronic media survey' that is their survey work gets printed in Newspapers and Magazines or it is relayed on Radio and Television. A general picture of this survey work is taken and then various Advertisements and Hoardings are made to publicize the survey work. These Advertisements are catchy with slogans and it has a piercing impact in the minds of peoples or masses. It generates a kind of craze in the minds of peoples and this makes them talk and further convince other peoples about such products, thus 'Corporate Psychology' is specially this craze in the minds of masses.

Today various sportsman, actors and actresses, Political Leaders and Reputed Personalities are a part of propaganda of these Corporate Giants round the globe. These Personalities are paid huge amount of money for the Advertisement films thus they become more like 'Brand Personalities'. Such personalities are like idols in the masses and when mass sees their idols in the Advertisement films of a product the masses are filled with an urge to use such products. Thus the products become a 'Hit' and peoples use this 'Hit' product almost throughout their life. 'Product Branding' is therefore a very important feature of Corporate Psychology.

Even in service units same strategy of 'Service Branding' is utilized and it makes a particular Doctor or a particular Hotel very famous. Masses visit a particular 'Service Provider' who is more famous. Masses visit a particular 'Service Provider' more for consultation because in their minds an impact is there that this 'Service Provider' is better from others. We also find that a particular school is having more students than other schools. All this is because if the 'services' of a particular organization is good then they become 'Hit' among the masses and then masses visit only these 'Service Hit' peoples and organizations.

In modern world therefore, the Corporate Psychology plays an important role in the minds of masses.

Chapter 17

Exploitation and Privatization

Corporate produce goods in mass scale to cater the needs of growing population. In order to achieve this aim of theirs', they are exploiting anything which they can think of. They exploit government, bureaucrats, employees, natural resources and wild life. Since they are very rich, so they fight various legal cases which crop up because of such exploitations and often such corporate are seen winning these cases. They even go to any extent polluting environment without bothering about its consequences. However, government and political world are not neglecting such kind of exploitation and many laws are made by government round the globe. Employees are exploited and such employees make trade unions to fight such exploitations of their owners. Various social organizations are coming up and many are established which fight these corporate exploitations. It is money world and corporate has money but because of various laws of government, today's corporate are changing their attitudes towards exploitations. They do not want a slur on their 'Corporate Brand' and so corporate are seen respecting and obeying all government laws related with employees, wild life and pollution. Exploitation is raising loud voices against it in all societies of world and so exploitation is getting tackled almost everywhere. However, in developing nations where awareness is shrouded in delusions, exploitations are on increase and many people are seen suffering. Employees have to work long hours and are seldom paid overtime salary, animals are slaughtered, child labor is seen with tentacles of bonded labor, salary payment is less compared to their work which means cheap labor and bribing for any fraudulent purpose are some of the exploitation scenario. Peoples are revolting against all forms of exploitation and soon exploitation will occupy a backseat in Corporate World. This exploitation is reaching in the Psychology of employees and they are raising voice against it in form of revolts.

Government is unable to pay salary to its employees in the fast changing World Scenario and so a new term 'Privatization' has come up in which most of the Government departments are going in the hands of Corporate World. Such organizations give a private design to such Government departments and employees put in their best services to gain good impressions. Such corporate pay good salary to its employees. Employees in such organizations are polite and have good behavior. They are good at convincing and their way of talking is very manipulative. Privatization is surely a boon to governments for their works gets handled by corporations of private sector. Government in return gets their tax from such private corporations. Seen in the privatization arena are Airways, Transport Companies, Shipping Corporations, Railways, Water and Electricity department, Industries making ancillaries of weapons and satellites. Privatization is therefore a global phenomenon. Many rich developed nations are privatized already.

Chapter 18

Mushroom Companies

In modern era of corporatism, everybody wants fame and big money in any manner which they can think. Peoples are opening small organizations to achieve their goal. Such small organizations which are cropping in any place with practically no infrastructure are called 'Mushroom Companies'. These companies are mostly on papers for getting government funds. They have few staff which is exploited by their employers.

Staff does not bother about exploitation because they are unaware of their world and they think that whatever their employers are saying – that is there work. Such mushroom companies, in order to survive, struggle for their existence. The employers and employees pose big to their customers while in reality they are basically nothing. They give false impression to their customers who are basically backward poor class of unaware masses. They come in big talks of such mushrooms and get deloused and pay money to buy services and goods of such companies. It is to be noted that such kind of 'Mushroom Companies' are more prevalent in villages and small towns where they can fool innocent masses. 'Mushroom Companies' are a worldwide phenomenon but in many developed nations, such mushroom companies do not exist. In developing nations, such mushroom companies have a very bad image and peoples are learning through their interactions with such companies. They are becoming aware about all fraudulent activities of such companies and fight to close such organizations. Even governments are realizing the nuisances which these mushroom companies are creating and are coming down with heavy axe on them.

In near future when illiterate masses of villages and false degree holders of small towns would become aware through media world and social organizations; then these mushroom companies will have no say in such masses and era of mushrooms will finish. Some mushroom companies which were properly managed and works, quality and quantity were strictly followed in their curriculum; these mushrooms have become big and today have made its place in corporate giants of the world. Mushroom companies can fool its staff and customers only to the extent till they are unaware. Once they become aware, it is for sure that such corporate organizations of mushroom nature would cease to exist. Many peoples' are delusional of corporate world and in such delusions they forget that they are unfit for corporate world. Yet they remain deloused and open such mushroom companies by arranging funds and the end result are that such owners of mushroom companies end in prison. Such deloused owners surely require the help of a Psychologist and if their delusions are serious natured then medical help of Psychiatrists are a must for them.

Chapter 19

Families of Corporate

In earlier times there was a prevalence of 'Joint Family System' in which two to three generation family members used to live under one roof. Then jobs and agriculture were in abundance and every member of family used to give his earnings in his house. Their family was the responsibility of whole house as such and members had very little say in their life. The Grandfather decisions used to be binding on Grand-children irrespective of the Parents and their feelings and emotions. This kind of Joint Family trend came to an end and today peoples in fast changing World have different desires and needs. Peoples or Society has thus developed a Psychology of fulfilling their desires which their Grandfather and joint family members can't understand.

The next scenario is that of 'Nuclear Family System' where Joint families have split to form three or four few members family. Such Nuclear families are prevalent even in today's society in

'Developing Nations' and to an extent in developed Nations. Such families have Father, Mother and their Children and Grandparents and other relatives have usually no say in their life.

In certain 'Developed Nations' of World where materialism is the essence in everybody's life, there is a trend of 'Broken Family System' in which Father, Mother, Brothers, sisters all earn and live independently. Usually in such families life is very complex and marriage and divorce is a common phenomenon.   Family   members consider each other as a burden, there are frequent family fights which may be among children, Mother – Children. Thus everybody quit their family and earn their own livelihood in such Broken Families.

There are families mostly 'Patriarchic', that is, father is the head of the family and takes all decisions. There are in many places, families as 'Matriarchal' that is, Mother is head and takes all decisions.

It is seen that big industrialists where money is in abundance, there is a tendency of 'Joint Family System'. However in salaried employees whether salary is lucrative or very less, there is a tendency of 'Nuclear Family' and 'Broken Family' where children after becoming independent and have an earning capacity leave their family and marry and have their own family.

Usually employees and service unit intellectuals have a disturbed family life and they can't pay all attention to their family. However, they have all attention of their family. Thus these employees have in their attitude a 'Burden Psychology' as per which they think that their wife or children are burden to them and want to settle their children as soon as they are of marriageable age. Certain employees whose salary is very lucrative, they give all facilities to their children and educate them in good schools. They are more successful in family life.

Chapter 20

General Scenario of Corporate World

Today conditions in Corporate World are far better than what it used to be in yester years. 'Developed Nations' has time regulations for employees work. In certain nations twenty four hours open office system with working hours been divided in shift has come up. Thus one shift employees complete their time schedule of work and then next shift employees take over. In 'Developing Nations' at many places five days a week working system is followed. All this has given ample time for workers to relax and overcome their fatigue.

Employees enjoy weekend holidays in many 'developed nations' by going on picnic tours, sightseeing, enjoying with their family, shopping, films, visiting friends and relatives or doing their personnel work and also culminating in their hobbies. In 'developing nations' usually means of enjoyment is limited to enjoying with their families or seldom go to shopping or sightseeing.

Discussions among employees of corporation and intellectuals of Service class; is mostly related to their profession or news which is related to their work. Family talks are seldom held and things like a good film, sexy actress, what acting; are also discussed in leisure hours. They also discuss property and vehicles. Any Government and new financial schemes also is not neglected by Corporate World.

Attitude of employees are very rare that they tend to abusive and unhealthy discussion. The corporate employees and service intellectuals basically are money minded and their discussions thus revolve round money as well.

Dressing Code and Sense of Hygiene is good in corporate employees and Service intellectuals. They are clean Gentlemen and Ladies and are well dressed and give a very good first impression. Even uneducated or less educated class of employee is well dressed and hygienic. Usually many Corporate Giants provide uniforms to its employees round the year.

The Corporate World provides polite and well behaved employees and intellectuals who mean business. Their World is limited to their office, House, friends and contacts. They don't have introvert tendencies and are open to everything and anything. They have a mixing tendency and are cooperative and a helping hand to their friends and colleagues.

Intellectuals of Corporate World are both Production Unit employees and

Service Unit peoples. These Intellectuals mean money to their Government. They are 'Human Resource' of a Nation and Nations round the globe are developing their 'Human Resource' in all fields and giving them welfare. If 'Human Resource' of a Nation is content then they will not leave their Nation and go to other Nations. 'Developing Nations' have realized this problem and are improving so that they do not lose their 'Human Resource' and there is no 'brain drain'.

ABOUT THE AUTHOR

After my education, I was fascinated by the corporate world. In my encounter with staffs and employers, I learnt that every corporate has its own Integrity. This integrity largely depended upon the type of employer and employees and the industrial relation that existed in the company. The machines in factories and employees in offices; all gave the decorum which a civilization needs in the Businesses through Corporate. My Book Corporate Psychology Company Traits is all about the decorum and the kind of interpersonal and intrapersonal relationships and various attires of the working force found in Corporate World. I with My Wife Mrs. Chandraprabha Wish Global Business Boom.

Thank You.

By –
Sanjeev Srivastava
5/356, Viram Khand – 5
Gomti Nagar
Lucknow (Uttar Pradesh)
INDIA

Cell No. →   +917985948892
E Mail Id →   sanchapra@gmail.com

www.ingramcontent.com/pod-product-compliance
Lightning Source LLC
Chambersburg PA
CBHW050915260726
48660CB00001B/213